I0123313

THE POWER OF

Love

AND

Forgiveness

JANEISHA HILL

JP PRODUCTION LTD.

©2019 by Janeisha Hill

©2019 JP Production Ltd.
The Power of Love and Forgiveness / Janeisha Hill

ISBN: 978-1-947671-43-0

All rights reserved. No part of this publication may be reproduced, distributed, or transmitted in any form or by any means, including photocopying, recording, or other electronic or mechanical methods, without the prior written permission of the publisher, except in the case of brief quotations embodied in critical reviews and certain other noncommercial uses permitted by copyright law. For permission requests, write to the publisher, addressed at the address below:

www.janeishahill.com

Ordering information for print editions:
Quantity sales. Special discounts are available on quantity purchases by corporations, associations, and others. For details, contact JP Production Ltd. via website address above.

Cover concept design: Janeisha Hill
Back cover and interior design: D.E. West / ZAQ Designs and Dust Jacket Creative Services

Printed in the United States of America

JP PRODUCTION LTD.

III

Table of Contents

Acknowledgements

I want to thank my heavenly Father for giving me the confidence to complete this book. It was very emotional at times, but with God's grace and mercy, I made it through.

I also want to take this opportunity to express my profound gratitude to all the people who offered input every step of the way. The blessings and motivation given by all were eye-opening, and all that I've received will surely take me a long way in the journey of life.

I would like to express my sincere gratitude to a very special person in my life, Mrs. Xavaunik Brown-Clarke, for all her support and many valuable contributions, all of which assisted me in completing this work.

Finally, I would like to thank my family and friends for their constant encouragement, without which this book would never have been possible.

Chapter One

"Youth is for the moment.
There is always time to grow old."

The sun ripened in the eastern sky and the university campus was silent in anticipation of the approaching summer break. It was the final class of the year. In Room 21, a classroom on the East Block, Rose-Marie sat, anxious to leave and see her friend Brian. She could hardly wait.

As the clock struck three, the entire campus erupted into a fit of ac-

tivity and students rushed from their classrooms.

"Summer time, here I come!" shouted one.

Brian wore a dark blue t-shirt and blue jeans. He stood at the front steps of the building, one foot up on the railing, and waited for Rose-Marie.

Rose-Marie was wearing a short, flared purple skirt and a yellow blouse. One breast peeked out as her heavy, single-strap black bag pulled the blouse slightly across her shoulder. When she saw Brian, Rose-Marie ran into his arms, giving him a hug and a kiss on the lips. He held her by the waist and guided her towards the car.

In the car, they talked about the function in the school auditorium that night. They'd both been invited, and Rose-Marie wanted to buy a dress at the mall to wear. So, Brian drove her there.

At the mall, Rose-Marie met up with two of her friends, Sharon and Donna. Walking around the shops, they started to gossip about another group of girls in their class. After chatting for a while, Rose-Marie eventually set about looking through and selecting dresses. She took a few into the fitting room, all of which she liked. Even though all the dresses suited her, she selected a short, sleeveless, black dress with a low back.

After buying the dress, Rose-Marie and her friends met up with Brian in the car park. Sharon and Donna said hello, then went on their way. Brian drove Rose-Marie home to get dressed for the event.

The fallen leaves danced on the roadway as Rose-Marie's sister, Dalia, skipped her way home from school. In the distance, one could see the landscape merging with the seashore, which

inspired a sense of rest and peacefulness. In the trees above, the birds sang melodiously, as if they were performing in a choir. The clouds were as fluffy as cotton candy, dancing around the deep blue sky and waving good-bye to the sinking sun.

Dalia arrived home and hugged her aunt.

"Good evening, Aunt Jackie."

After greeting her aunt, Dalia ran into her room and took off her blue jeans and pink shirt. Instead, she put on a pink Barbie blouse and went back down to her aunt, who was busy making crafts for a friend's wedding. When Dalia went down to see her, Aunt Jackie paused her work to prepare a small plate of macaroni and cheese with baked beans and sliced sausage for her niece. Dalia ate quickly and was excited to watch her aunt continue making her crafts.

As Aunt Jackie was explaining what she was working on, Rose-Marie and Bri-

an arrived. Brian escorted Rose-Marie to the front door, kissed her on the forehead and told her that he would pick her up at 6:30 p.m. He waited until she was safe inside, then returned to his car and drove off.

Rose-Marie entered the house, and was greeted by Dalia, who ran to her and jumped in her arms.

"Marie, you're home!" she squealed.

With a big smile, Rose-Marie kissed her head and placed her back down on her chair.

"What did you bring home for me?" Dalia prodded.

"Shhh!" Rose-Marie whispered. "You'll get it later."

Rose-Marie greeted her aunt and went upstairs to her room with her bags. Once inside, she leaned against the door, shutting it with her back. She sighed. Placing her bags on the bed, she

checked the clock on the wall. The time was 5:45 p.m. She did not have much time, so she quickly tied her hair up and rushed in the shower. She turned on the faucet and the water came in full force, beating against her body. In no time, Rose-Marie was clean and out of the shower, wrapped in a soft, fluffy towel. She gave her face a few extra splashes, grabbed a face towel, and wiped it dry.

Back in her bedroom, Rose-Marie took her black dress out of the shopping bag and unwrapped it. Holding it against her body, she stood in front of the mirror, blushing. She put it on, then went to the closet and grabbed a pair of black, high-heeled shoes to highlight her red nail polish. While she styled her hair, Brian called to let her know that he was just five minutes away. She finished her hair and put on her accessories, took one last look in the mirror, and went downstairs.

Aunt Jackie and Dalia looked admiringly at her and smiled.

"Wow, Marie! You look great!" Dalia exclaimed.

Just then, the doorbell rang. It was Brian. As Rose-Marie opened the door, he let a out a gasp , took her hand and escorted her to the car. Within moments, they were on their way, chatting as they drove along.

The college parking lot was completely full, and cars were piling up to get inside. Brian managed to drive up close to the auditorium to let Rose-Marie out. While he went to find a parking spot, she went inside to find seats for both of them.

Finally, he arrived and sat down beside her, throwing his arms gently around her shoulders, embracing her. The room was buzzing with activity. People were talking with one another,

laughing and getting excited for what was to come.

Suddenly, there a hush fell over the crowd as the Vice President made her way to the podium. She briefly introduced the guest speaker. The crowd applauded politely as the guest speaker made her way onto the stage and over to the podium.

"I am overwhelmed to be here with all of you, to share my relationship experiences."

This was how she began her story.

Chapter Two

"I am the masterpiece of God and
I am designed for success."

In the garden of Brandford, a little flower bloomed among her three brothers and three sisters. She had curly, dark, long, thick hair. Her dark brown eyes sparkled like sun beams. She had an arrow-straight nose, and thin lips, and always wore a pleasant smile. Her skin was like caramel, smooth and soft. Her name was Jamie Black.

I come from a highly loved and respected family. My father was a Christian minister, and was very successful. He was a very strict, God-fearing minister. Because of his generosity and wisdom, he had earned the respect of most, if not all, the people in our community. He loved everyone. My mother was a house wife, raising children and supporting of my dad's work.

Her hair was curly, black, and thick, like mine. She was a gentle soul with very small feet. She was not well educated, but was still one of the wisest women I knew. She was always there for our family, was very supportive of all our aspirations, and made us her top priority.

She always told us two things, "Aim for the sky," and "fear God."

For years during my childhood, my mother was sick, but she still took care of

her household, and she was always there when we needed advice.

Her greatest wish was to see her me and her youngest son, Darren, achieve a career before she died, and she prayed for it every day. In the end, she got her wish. And may her soul rest in peace.

We grew up in a small district called Long Bay, in Jamaica. As kids, we called it St. Patrick Avenue because it seemed to add a little class to the neighbourhood.

In our family, older siblings were not allowed to hit the smaller ones, but instead had to seek the help of our parents if we couldn't settle our differences alone. I really liked that rule. We were not rich by any means, but were somehow seen as being rich because of our high standards and morals.

We were taught to love God first. We had to respect the elderly, no matter

whether they were rich or poor. We could attend church freely, but were monitored in any other activity. I was proud of my upbringing. I was who I was because of my parents and my siblings. I was thankful. My mom and dad also raised my nephew, Mark, and my niece, Mya, both of whom we all adored.

Chapter Three

*"Success is nothing without having
someone to share it with."*

Between the ages of six and thirteen I attended Bogue View All Ages School. Then, from thirteen to seventeen I studied at Arnold High School. During that time, I attended the Church of the Nazarene. My best friends were the Campbell's: Yanika, Valrie, Calvin (Cal), Jana (Reds), and Pamela (Tippa). We grew up together, went to the same church and schools,

but they left for Canada in the '70s. Before they left, a girl named Mary Coke joined our group of friends, so when the Campbells moved away, we became closer, even though she attended a different school.

Nowadays, we are all in Canada and we call each other occasionally to reminisce the good old days. We all have different lifestyles and different friends, but when we talk on the phone or meet up with each other, we realize that we still have that bond.

I went to Montego Bay in 1973, where I was employed by the Jamaica Youth Service as a recreation officer. I worked for six months before transferring into the education system, where I taught for three years. I was great at my job, even though I knew I did not want to make it my career.

I lived with my sister Ingrid and her family during that time. We all attended

the Wesleyan Holiness Church, and
I became very active in the church community. It was a great time in my life.

Wesleyan was under the leadership
of Pastor Wright. He was a young, kind,
honorable, stern, but modern minister,
who was loved by all. He made everyone feel special. To our surprise, he died
suddenly in February 1982 from a brain
tumor. May his soul rest in peace.

From 1977 to 1980, I attended
the Cornwall School of Nursing, and
boarded at the student nursing residence. There, I had a roommate, named
Evette Blake, who became a wonderful
friend. Together, we set an example for
our batch mates. We were the perfect
roommates. Any disagreement would be
worked out amicably, and we were both
tidy and skilled in the kitchen. We were
both very independent, but never took
one another for granted. After graduat-

ing, we continued to live at the residence, and continued to be best friends until I left for Canada.

While attending Wesleyan Holiness Church, I met a guy named Mark, with whom I had a relationship for seven years. He made me happy, and made my transition from the country to the big city easy. My parents and other family members were not very impressed with him, but that did not stop me. His family really liked my company, and treated me as their own.

One night, though, I found out that Mark was in several relationships with different women at once, and was just trying to keeping it a secret. That night, I cried so hard. My heart pounded hard, and the timing was very bad because I was in the middle of my final year examination.

Mark's excuse was that I did not give him any attention. He apologized several

times in several ways, but I was strong and refused to give in because I loved and respected myself.

I remembered confiding with Pastor Wright before he died. He thought I could give it another chance. I cannot forget telling him that as much as I loved Mark, I would not get back together with him.

I thanked God for giving me the strength, even in those youthful years, to be strong and wise. I also have my parents to thank for my strong foundation, and my older siblings for the good examples they set.

Being a child of God was very important to me. I attended both Wesleyan Holiness and the Church of the Nazarene, which was in the big city, where my sisters, Ingrid and Lorna, attended and my other siblings and my parents attended the other church branches.

I enjoyed going to church, and a group of us from Cornwall Regional Hospital (CRH) would visit each other's churches.

Pastor Thompson was always very kind. I will always remember that when there was a strike at the hospital cafeteria, he brought me food to eat.

I continued dating, but on a more casual basis. I was almost in my mid twenties when three men fell for me all at once. I had shown interest in each of them, but had openly told them that I did not want any serious relationship, and was also seeing other people.

It turned out that my husband was one of those guys. At the time, ours was a long-distance relationship and we spoke frequently by phone. I felt that I could tell him anything. He was my friend, and I have a wonderful story about how we met.

Chapter Four

"If it's going to be, it's up to me."

In 1980, immediately after graduation, I worked on the surgical floor at Cornwall Regional Hospital. There, I was assigned to a patient, Brenda Gardner, who was in her sixties. She had been diagnosed with a tumor in the vertebral column after battling breast cancer and having a mastectomy ten years earlier.

I was kind to Brenda, as I was with all my patients. She was in severe pain

as she went into surgery to have a laminectomy. She knew how risky the surgery was, but also knew her prognosis was poor and it was one of the only options. As she prepared for the surgery, I took the time to talk to her and listen to her fears. During my daily care of her, she told me that she had a son who she knew would like me.

One day, Brenda took my right hand with both of her hands, and looked in my eyes.

"I would like for you to meet with my son, Bobby," she said, sincerely.

I smiled, "I am already involved in a long-term relationship with someone I will eventually marry."

Still, Brenda began telling all the nurses, doctors, and family members who came to visit her that I was her daughter-in-law. She would call me at the residence

on my day off if she wanted to talk or needed anything. She became extremely attached to me.

One day during visiting hours, when I was attending to her, her daughters entered the room. She was so excited to see them. I was about to step away after tucking her into bed, but she grabbed my hands pulling me towards her. She introduced her daughters, Diana and Caroline. They lived in Canada, but had traveled to be with her during her illness. Brenda's daughters were very friendly, and after seeing them a few times at the hospital, I invited Diana to sleep in the nurse's residence with me, so that she could be closer to her mother.

I introduced Diana to my then-fiancé.

"He is nice, but my brother is nicer," she said.

I smiled, turned my head to the side, and rolled my eyes.

I was not interested in another relationship, and never asked any further questions about her brother.

I continued caring for Brenda. In the days prior to her surgery, we spoke at length, and I wished her good luck and God's blessing. She survived the surgery, but unfortunately died suddenly post-operation from embolism. May her soul rest in peace.

I was at the nurse's residence one evening when I was called down to the reception desk to take a call. It was Mrs. Gardner's daughter on the phone in tears.

"Mama died!" she cried.

My heart was broken, and I hung up quickly. I did not attend the funeral, but went to see Caroline afterwards to express my sympathy. She lived in Grange Hill, where she had a hair salon. She, along with her brother-in-law, George Barrett,

took me up to their home, where I visited her grave. As I stood over her yellow, pink and white tomb, I whispered a soft prayer.

After I left the graveside, I met her son, Bobby, at the family house. He was dressed in a pair of black pants and blue shirt, neatly tucked in.

He invited me to talk with him outside the house.

"I have heard so much about you, and I would like us to start a relationship."

"I am already in a committed relationship," I replied.

He said, "Well, we can be friends."

I visited the family one more time before they left for Canada.

After Bobby left, he started calling me at least three times per week. Our conversations were sometimes serious, sometimes very entertaining. At the same time, I was having major prob-

lems in my other relationship, and Bobby would listen to me and even encourage me. He was really caring, understanding, and genuinely interested in what I was going through. I began to feel that we were soul mates.

In the summer of 1981, I visited Canada to see him and his sisters, as well as Maldon and all the Campbells. We connected there, and I knew I wanted to see him in person again.

Christmas of 1981, Bobby visited Jamaica and we went on a lot of dates.

One night, we went out to a restaurant called the Pelican Grill in Montego Bay. We had dinner and cuddled in the restaurant for a while. They were playing a song that I liked on the stereo, and I started to rock back and forth on the chair. While I moved, Bobby took me by the hand and we stood. He put his arm around my waist and held me tight. We danced

for a while. Everybody was watching us because we must have seemed very in love. Suddenly, Bobby knelt down and reached into his pocket. He took out a black ring box and opened it.

"Will you marry me?" he said.

"Yes, I will!" I said, smiling broadly.

Still, deep in my mind, I was scared.

I blushed as he slipped the ring onto my finger.

As I mentioned, I was dating two other guys at the time, but found Bobby to be most understanding and the kindest of them all. There was so much good in him.

"My parents would have to give their approval for marriage," I said later.

He agreed to speak to my parents about our union.

I had not told anyone in my family about the relationship, only my friend Edith and Pastor Wright.

While Bobby was in Jamaica, my mother got sick and had to be hospitalized. In her room at the hospital, I told her about him. A few months earlier, Caroline had visited her and mentioned the relationship. At that time, my mother had confronted me, and I had told her that it was nothing serious. My mother was the kind of woman who would give you advice even when you didn't want it.

After the proposal, Bobby went to Cornwall Region Hospital and visited my mother.

He spoke with her, and asked her for her blessing, and for my hand in marriage. She gave him her blessing, but told him, "You have to see and speak to her father for the request to be complete."

Bobby liked my mother and was anxious, but nervous to meet my father. I decided to accompany him to see my dad. I introduced them, and without hesitation Bobby asked, "Can I have your

blessing to have your daughter's hand in marriage?"

"Yes," my father said.

He offered his blessings, then proceeded to give us his words of advice. He told us that he would pray for us.

As soon as the conversation was over, Bobby left as quickly as possible, so my dad didn't have a chance to change his mind.

We continued to correspond and call one another, until Bobby invited me to Canada, where we'd planned to marry. I took a leave of absence from my job and informed my parents, siblings, and close friends of my intention.

Chapter Five

"*In any moment of decision,
the best thing you
can do is the right thing.
The worst thing
you can do is nothing.*"

By this time, I had learned that Bobby had been married once before, and had two children by his former wife. But I was too committed, and Bobby was such a gentleman, I couldn't give up the opportunity.

I told Bobby that I would come to live with him in Canada for five years, after which we could move back to Jamaica, as he had told me he eventually wanted to do.

I cannot help but remember the last time I spoke with Dad before leaving for Canada.

"Are you certain about this marriage?" he asked.

"Dad," I replied. "Any marriage is a big gamble. I am just putting this in the hands of the Lord."

I arrived in Canada in May of 1982. I had already started to make plans for the wedding when Bobby said to me, "Jamie, the divorce isn't completed yet."

This made me upset, as I felt I was wasting my time coming to Canada if we weren't going to be married. But by the end of summer 1982, Bobby had his di-

vorce papers in order, and we set a date for October of that year.

His two children lived in Jamaica with their Aunt Caroline, and their mother also lived there with her father.

At that time, I was still in love with Bobby, but becoming a bit discouraged. As I found out more and more about him, I became slightly concerned. Still, we discussed our problems openly. I told him all the things about him that I could not live with, one of which was his smoking.

"J, I will quit the smoking if you marry me," he promised.

One month before our wedding, Bobby got a job at an automotive store. I was so happy for him because he had been out of work for more than a year.

Veronica and Kevin, his sister and brother-in-law, were very supportive

throughout the whole process leading up to the wedding day. They worked hard on the guest list and helped us make all the arrangements.

The night before the wedding, Everette decorated the hall along with some friends. Then, on the actual day of the wedding, she did the bridesmaids' hair and Kevin played the music for the ceremony. Two of my friends from Jamaica and one from the United States attended the ceremony, along with my best childhood friends, the Campbell's and Maldon.

The wedding was lovely. I felt pretty and well-loved, and was hardly nervous at all. I was sure that my family was thinking of me, and sending special prayers up to heaven for us.

My sister Lorna had wanted to attend the wedding, but I'd discouraged her from coming, because my Canadian lifestyle was

new to me, and I did not think she would approve.

"Mom isn't well and I cannot assist financially; therefore, I don't want you to spend extra money to attend the wedding."

"I understand," she said.

In the months before the wedding, I had prayed day and night that everything would work out well. I was nervous and somewhat confused by the whole situation. I even went to the travel agency and made reservations to return home just one week before the wedding, but could not bring myself to do it. Eventually, I was able to confide in my brother, Gavin, who was attending teachers' college. I told him all about Bobby's history, and pleaded with him.

"Gavin, please do not to tell anyone. I feel like I've failed my family."

Bobby promised me a honeymoon in Jamaica as soon as he was financially stable, but we could not go anywhere after the wedding.

My girlfriends spent three weeks with me after the wedding, helping me to settle in with Bobby and trying to keep my encouraged. Still, there came a time soon after the wedding when I was desperate for a job. I took the Canadian nursing exam, which I failed the first time around. Afterwards, I studied hard, learning about Canadian food and culture, and by the time I took the exam again, I passed with an almost perfect score.

By December 1982, I was missing my home and my family. Christmas was not the same. There were lots of activities and my in-laws tried to accommodate me, but something was missing. I tried my best to be happy, but I felt crazy without a job,

and without my friends and family. I wanted freedom, and my own money.

In February 1983, immigration finally gave me a work permit. But at that time, there was a recession, and no one was interested in hiring a nurse with landed immigrant status, especially one that was new in the country with nothing more than a simple work permit. I felt miserable and frustrated.

Bobby had no idea what I was going through. I constantly felt like I was in his territory, invading his privacy. He started going out on Friday nights, and then on Sundays, he would go to visit his sister or go away with friends. Meanwhile, I would be at the house, all alone. Sometimes on Sundays I would make baked chicken, vegetables, pasta and rice and peas. I would decorate the table with the food and wait for him to arrive; but he'd come in the door having already eaten at his sister's. It felt strange to have him be inconsiderate with me. It was not the Bobby I had come to know.

We had lots of arguments in and out of the house, and he showed me little respect in public. We would go to parties together, where he would sit me down at a table and go off to the bar, whispering in women's ears and touching their bodies. I would be left in the corner to watch him flirting with these girls, and it made me extremely upset. Still, I never thought he was a cheater. I spoke to his sisters about his behavior, but they soon became tired of my constant whining. I could not help it, though, because all my family was in Jamaica.

Chapter Six

*"Character is a simple habit
long continued."*

In March of 1983, I got a job at a nursing agency in Toronto. I was elated, because by that point I was homesick and felt ready to throw in the towel. The day after I got the job, I started working, and I lost sixteen pounds in two weeks from rushing around. I was not familiar with Toronto's subway sys-

tem, or with the general employment system in Canada.

Often, I would be called to work from 3 p.m. until 11 p.m. and had nowhere to stay after finishing the shift. Bobby gave me numbers for some family and friends downtown, and I would move from home to home, depending on which family I could stay with on a given night. Eventually, I began staying in a boarding house for fifteen dollars a night. I would go from hospitals to nursing homes, to retirement homes on the subway, with directions from the agency. In order to work, I took the bus from our home in Kitchener into Toronto, which was just over an hour in one direction.

Bobby's kids were brought to Canada from Jamaica. From friends in Jamaica, I had heard a lot of negative things about the treatment of the children. I could not believe that children of decent parents

would be treated badly and made to suffer.

The children's names were Raymond and Ray. I found it hard to juggle working in Toronto and taking care of them, but I had a good babysitter who lived in our apartment building and the boys were very well behaved. They clearly loved each other, and would always find the smallest chair in any room and sit together on it. They never fought and were always polite.

By the time they arrived, Raymond was seven years old and had not even begun to learn the absolute basics. He was shy, quiet, and appeared somehow sad at all times. I had to attend his school at least once a week because his teacher wanted to discuss his learning problem. I worked together with this teacher, trying to be supportive until he started learning. He hated his books and was

very angry with me for pushing him to study. Because of this, I had a bad start with him, but he was angry with everyone except his brother, Ray.

Ray was three years old. He was cheerful, happy, and called me "Mom" from the first day we met. We had a true parent-child relationship.

Raymond, on the other hand, always called me "Jamie."

I never told either of them what to call me, but after a period of time, Raymond also began calling me "Mom."

One afternoon, I sat them down together and told them that although I wanted to be a mother to them, I was only their father's wife and not their real mother. I told them not to feel pressured into calling me their mother. Still, I was happy because they were the only children I had.

When I worked in Toronto, I saved

my money so that I didn't have to de-
pend on Bobby for additional support.
We were good at working together, financially. We built up sufficient savings
to make a down payment on our first
house together in November of 1984,
the same month my mother died in
Jamaica.

On November 24, the very same
weekend that I was to move into my
new house, I got a call from my nephew
informing me that my mother had died.
This was traumatic, because I knew
I would I never get the chance to do
what I really wanted to do for her. I was
grateful, at least, that Bobby and I had
spent the previous Christmas in Jamaica
with her. While I attended her funeral
in Jamaica, Bobby, with the help of his
sisters and friends, moved into our new
house. When I returned, everything was
in order.

Chapter Seven

*"The broken becomes
the master of mending"*

My problems with my in-laws started when Diana separated from her husband and moved to Kitchener from their home in Alberta. After arriving, she started hanging out with one of her brother's girlfriends in Toronto.

At around the same time, Bobby's brother told him he had heard from someone in Toronto that I was planning

on leaving him as soon as I got my papers in order. Bobby confronted me, accusing me of being untrustworthy. This hurt me badly. I felt cheap and was disappointed that he had believed such a lie. I had just invested all my savings to buy a house with him, and here he was making my life miserable with his false accusations.

The thought of leaving had never crossed my mind, and such words never crossed my lips.

With every disagreement, Bobby nagged me with this same story.

Sasha, the girl who Diana socialized with in Toronto, was starting to tell the family many different stories of what I had supposedly said about them. This caused some problems because although they all knew me personally, they seemed to choose to believe the gossip in Toronto.

I cried often and vowed to leave everything to God. Several weeks later,

I was told that this same girl was trying to desperately to pull me away from the family because she was having an affair with my sister-in-law's boyfriend, who was already married.

One day, my sister-in-law called, accusing me of spreading gossip about Sasha, which was ridiculous. Sasha, who had consistently harassed me, had two kids with my sister-in-law's boyfriend while they were still communicating and she did not know. I found it amazing that someone could manipulate another person to that degree. My sister-in-law eventually revealed the whole story to me, confessing that no one could ever take my name to her again. I know this was quite embarrassing for her. However, that did not stop her from being a thorn in my flesh.

Working at Kitchener Walton Hospital (KWH) was an eye-opener

for me. I had worked at many different health facilities in Toronto, but in every place I worked, there were always many nurses from different backgrounds, and we all saw our differences as an advantage. But at KWH, approximately 98% of registered nurses were white. Most black workers were either practical nurses or housekeeping staff, and there were no blacks in supervising positions. I had the feeling that many of them resented having a black registered nurse in charge. It led to complaints to our nurse manager regarding my being "antisocial." This was all they could complain about, since there was never any issue with my professional conduct.

I clearly remembered the day, three months after my employment date, when my supervisor called me into her office. I was expecting to be fired. I was so scared. She told me the girls had come to her as

a group to complain about me, and she went on to list the complaints.

My first question was, "Did they complain about the quality of my work?"

She said, "No. The only problem is that you ask for help with simple things."

"I am new, and this is the way I am accustomed to working," I replied. "In dealing with patients, I cannot afford any error; therefore, I must ask questions until I feel comfortable at this new institution."

I told her that I was tired of hearing gossip from the girls, who were always ready to talk about anyone who was not actually at their table. I said that every group I went to break with had negative things to say about her in particular. I told her that if I had not been open-minded, the girls' gossip would have made me think worse of her, but that

I had a personal approach of evaluating everyone on my own terms.

"I really appreciate talking with you," she said. "Now, I know where you are coming from and I respect your thinking."

From that day on, the supervisor and I had a great relationship until the time she resigned.

Chapter Eight

"Turn your wounds into wisdom."

My sons seemed very comfortable approaching me first whenever they needed something. At a young age, they had been sent off to live in Jamaica with their aunt. Their real mother, as I mentioned, lived there with her father. I was told she was mentally unstable and that the children were suffering, so I suggested that they be brought to live with us. I was happy

to have them, but still wanted children of my own.

In 1984, around the time I began working at KWH, I decided it was time to start a family. We tried for a few years without success.

The whole situation made me very upset, but Bobby was neither supportive nor understanding. In 1987, I went to my family doctor, Dr. Atkinson, and I told her about my problem with infertility, and the fact that I was miserable at home. She introduced me to the Fertility Clinic in London, where I did a tubal inflation and several other tests. Everything came back normal.

The doctors could not understand why I was not getting pregnant, so the doctor ordered a sperm count on Bobby. He then did a biopsy of the testes to assess the sperm count more precisely, and discovered that they were very low. When

they gave me the news that he would not be able to father my kids, I felt incredibly lonely. Meanwhile, Bobby was still going out, behaving irresponsibly. In those days, he was no longer interested in discussing my feelings.

Seeing how desperate I was, Dr. Atkinson told me about artificial insemination, which we then decided to try. The procedure meant going to London three to five days per cycle and doing bloodwork for two to four days in Kitchener. Prior to that, I would give myself fertility injections six to eight days per month. The whole procedure took a year and nine months, and I had two pregnancies that ended in miscarriages. It was a very traumatic and painful time, and I had to keep everything secret. I did not want to hurt Bobby's ego, so I kept it from his family and friends.

I traveled to London by myself and went through all the emotions alone. The drug had numerous side effects, and Bobby was not tolerant of me. If I even hinted at being moody, he would become very angry with me. I wanted to die.

At that point, his sister actually cursed me, telling me I could not have children because I "dash wey belly". I thought my husband would have told his family that it was his problems, that were preventing us from conceiving. Instead, he allowed me to be cursed in public. I felt very sad, lonely, and miserable. As I got more and more depressed, I began to seek counselling.

Because our marriage was in a constant state of conflict, we had already been through some counselling. I knew that Bobby loved me, but that he had difficulty respecting and caring for women. Because I knew he loved me, I decided

to fight to keep my marriage alive, but his family's interference did not make things easier for me. Each time we had an argument, he would go to their house, and then return, not wanting to discuss our problems.

Often, when we had disagreements, he would leave and go to his sister's place. One time, he left and didn't return. I knew she had to go to work the following morning, and became very concerned. At 3 a.m., I called his sister.

"Have you seen Bobby?" I asked.

She replied, "No."

I had to be at work at seven in the morning, but never slept a wink. The next day, someone told me that Bobby had indeed been at his sister's house when I'd called. I felt betrayed. I confronted her about it, but although we spoke civilly, nothing was truly resolved.

Chapter Nine

*"The successful man keeps moving.
They make mistakes,
but they never quit."*

I remembered going to my husband's family reunion in Jamaica, prepared to have a good time, but was attacked by my sister-in-law during our stay. She was angry with my husband because he paid too much attention to me, and she wanted to fight me over it. I had never been involved in such a scene in my life. All the other family mem-

bers took her side and kept their distance from us.

Bobby and I continued to have our ups and downs, but stayed together.

At a New Year's party, my sister-in-law decided it was time to make peace with me. Despite her previous behavior, I hugged her and instantly reunited with her. From that point, relations with his family were decent, until Bobby's cousin decided to bring her kids to Canada from Jamaica.

Apparently, his cousin told my oldest sister-in-law that she had asked her to take care of the kids. We had no idea. When the lady called and asked us to keep the children until she got a permanent place for them, I agreed.

This angered my sister-in-law, who stopped speaking to me. Apparently, she thought that because the parents were rich in Jamaica, I was being paid to have

the kids. But she eventually got over it, and started talking to me again.

After this, Bobby's family and I went through a positive period where we would meet up and play poker three to four times a week. We had a great time.

Bobby and I continued to argue, seemingly always in conflict with each other. His children didn't seem happy, and would no longer speak to me. Raymond was either shy or angry. Ray was quiet most of the time, but would still be affectionate with me at times.

I was missing my family in Jamaica more than ever.

I re-evaluated my life frequently. I was so unhappy, and the kids looked unhappy too. Bobby was the happiest, because if there was a problem, he would simply leave home and spend time with his family or friends. I thought to myself that I had no right dictating to a person how to live. The truth was that Bobby was not happy with my lifestyle, and I was not happy with his. We could not manage to meet each other halfway. He never listened when I expressed my sadness about the problem of not having a child or about the miscarriages. I had no one to talk to when I was down, while he happily ran away to his family.

In September of 1993, Bobby and I had another disagreement. It was simple, as they usually were. We had been invited to a wedding the following Saturday for one of my coworkers. Bobby was going to be working overtime that weekend. I told him that I would go to the church alone at noon, and then we would go to the reception together in the evening, after he returned home from work.

I went to get my hair done at his sister's and she asked me why Bobby would not go to the church. I told her that the

ceremony was only thirty minutes and he didn't want to miss work, and that we would attend the reception together. I found her question unusual at the time, but didn't realize what was really behind it. Afterwards, Bobby went to work and I went to church. I was home by 1:30 p.m. and got his clothes prepared. By 7:30 p.m., he still had not come home, and I began worrying that something might be wrong.

I started to get dressed and kept a lookout for him. By 8 p.m., he still was not home.

I got Ray to called his Aunt Verona's house at 8:30 p.m. Sure enough, he was there.

I was furious. I took off my dress clothes and stayed home.

Bobby did not return until 3 a.m. When he arrived, he did not mention a single thing about the wedding or say

where he had been, or why he was home so late.

Finally, I asked him why he had never showed up for the reception. He responded coldly, with the same excuse that had been hidden in his sister's earlier question.

"It's funny that you went to the church alone and still wanted me to go to the reception with you."

I was shocked. We had discussed the whole thing, and I knew that he hadn't wanted to miss work for a half-hour ceremony.

Chapter Ten

"A good friend is one who
knows everything about you
and still likes you."

I was angry and decided that night I could not go on living like that. I lay in bed, but could not sleep.

The following Monday, I had a very rough day at work, and spent much of the time praying for my shift to end. Driving home, reality hit me. Arriving home, I only wanted to be back at work.

I suddenly realized that I wanted a place of love and peace to go home to at the end of a long day of work, even if there was no one there to greet me. The next day I went to work, and immediately started looking for apartments.

I said nothing to anyone, but found somewhere that I liked. I made all the arrangements by myself, spending extra time reading the Bible and praying. I could feel that I had made the right decision.

The following Saturday morning, I had a talk with Raymond and Ray. I sat with them in the living room, and explained to them that I was very unhappy and was going to move out. I told them that I could not get along with their dad, and that none of it was their fault. I told them that I would be there for them if they needed me, and I was expecting them to come and spend time with me

whenever they wished. I gave them by phone number.

I told Bobby about my plans that same evening. I told him of my unhappiness, and that I could no longer live that way. He became very angry and cursed me, disrespecting my family and me.

With every word he spoke, the thought of leaving made me happier and happier. I did not bother to even answer him.

The following days and nights, he would curse me regularly. Whenever he started, I would simply go for a walk, regardless of the time.

I told all this to my one friend, Sofia, and she was very supportive of me. She had discouraged the move, but wanted me to be happy.

I called one of my sisters-in-law and told her that I had something I

wanted to talk to the family about, and would prefer to do it in a group with the sisters. I suggested they named a meeting place. She agreed to speak with them, but soon got back to me with the news that they had decided not to meet with me. I tried to remain calm, though inside I was tormented.

Shortly before moving, I went to clean the new apartment by myself. On the way home, someone hit the back end of my car. My car was totally written off. I was angry and left with a head injury. Bobby took me to the hospital when the police came to see me.

Because of the injury, I was off from work, and slowly packed up all my stuff. Bobby and I decided together what things I could take. With much insistence from me, he allowed me to take a bedroom set and a dining room set, nothing more.

The day of the move came, and my new phone was installed. Sofia helped me with everything, as I was still struggling with my injury. My head was still bandaged, and I could hardly walk. I had not wanted anyone to help with the move, because I knew that Bobby and the family would have been rude to them; but Sofia insisted that she did not want me to do it alone. I had planned to move while the boys were at school, so they wouldn't have to watch me leave.

Before moving, Diana, Bobby's sister, called me. I told her that I was moving out, and she came over immediately.

"If you and Bobby are unhappy, then you are doing the right thing. I am happy for you," she said, hugging me and crying.

Shortly after, I called Bobby's sister, Caroline, to tell her that I was moving.

She then called Bobby at work to tell him to go home immediately and prevent me from moving everything. Then, someone from his work called me, telling me to be careful. I felt exhausted, and like everyone was out to get me.

By the time I actually left the house, Bobby had stopped constantly cursing me. We could talk, and he even helped to move a few boxes and the bed frame. Still, he was telling his family a different story, so they were all angry with me. At that time, Bobby was saying all manner of evil things to his sisters and friends about me. There was a lot of gossip going around, and I would often get phone calls from people telling me to be careful. But I just read my Bible, prayed, went to church, and ignored the scandal.

Chapter Eleven

*"The Lord I serve is bigger
than my problems and
there is nothing impossible
for Him."*

After I moved, all Bobby's sisters started giving me the cold shoulder. I would say hello to them each time I saw them. Some would answer, others would not. Ray called me daily when his father was out, but Raymond would ignore me when he saw me and never called me. At first, I tried to call

him and keep the lines of communication open, but I stopped when I saw him at a function and he refused to acknowledge me.

Immediately after moving, I had to buy a car. The accident had left me without a vehicle. Bobby offered to drive me to the dealership, where I decided to buy a Red Cavalier. After I arrived home, I was told that my oldest sister-in-law, Pam, was in the hairdressing shop complaining about how silly Bobby was to be helping me buy a car. I sent a text message, informing them that I had bought the car with my own money, and that Bobby didn't even have to co-sign the lease.

Bobby and I managed to maintain a civil relationship after I left. I still gave him money to assist with the mortgage payments, and he would sometimes visit me at my apartment. However, he still

seemed to be telling his family and friends lies about me, while he simultaneously came to me complaining about them. When he tried to tell me about his problems with them, I would shut him down, saying I didn't want to hear anything negative about them.

Despite living separate lives, we continued to have disagreements that would routinely get out of hand. The biggest problem we had revolved around a computer that I had bought for work. I told him that I was going to take the computer, and he made a huge fuss about it, complaining to his family that I wanted to take the computer from his children.

Even after starting my new independent life, people kept telling me all the things Bobby and his family were saying about me, and I began feeling that I needed to just get away from

them completely. The family told people I thought I was more educated than they were, and that I compared my car to theirs, and so on. Bobby even began calling my friends and telling them nasty things that I had supposedly said about them.

One friend, Marsha, simply replied, "Jamie is my friend, so don't bring any more of your scandals to me."

Bobby had done his best to alienate me from everyone, but Marsha was not going to forsake me.

"In the name of Jesus," she said to him, "get thee behind me."

Another friend of ours threw Bobby out of her house because of the way he talked about me, and because he said that the kids didn't like me because I hadn't treated them right. The friend said that she could not listen to him anymore, and told him to leave.

In March of 1994, I decided to go on a vacation to Jamaica with my girl-friend, Lorrie. I told Bobby about it. By that point, he had started drinking a lot, and he continued to be very disloyal to me. He told so many lies, and would just go around from house to house with the kids, telling lies about me. When I refused to let him visit me at my apart-ment, he took it hard and began drink-ing even more.

A week before my trip, Ray called and asked if I could come home. He said that his dad needed me, and that they all wanted me to come back. That was the first time that they had ever expressed such a thing. I thought about it all night, but I decided that I would not expose myself to that kind of abuse again.

Another evening, Ray called to tell me that his dad was ill. This was at 10

p.m. My cousin, Mike, was living with me at that time. God must have seen my loneliness and sent me one of the best roommates I could have had in such desperate time. I told Ray that I would not come to the house because I thought his father was faking the illness. I had come to the conclusion that Bobby's family only wanted to make my life miserable, and that I wanted nothing more to do with it. But later that night, Ray called me a second time. This time was at 2 a.m., from the hospital. He told me that his dad had been admitted, but I still did not want to go. I knew that his family would certainly be there, and that they would not want me there. Ray called me a third time, but I still refused to go. At 6 a.m., unable to sleep, I called the hospital to confirm that he had been admitted, and I went to see him. When I arrived, the boys were by his side.

Chapter Twelve

*"Living in the past, paralyses
the present and bankrupts the future."*

When I arrived, both boys left the room without saying a word. I wanted to believe they were happy that I came to relieve them.

I went with Bobby to the x-ray department. Afterwards, the doctor told us that he had an ulcer and would require surgery. I told Bobby that I would get a phone from the nursing station, so

that he could let his sisters know that he was going into the operating room, but he refused. So it was I who saw him off as he went in for surgery.

With tears in his eyes, he asked, "Will you be here when I return?"

"Yes," I replied. "And I will be praying for you."

I cried all the way to his house.

I was going to be leaving for Jamaica in a few days, so I got Bobby's personal belongings together for his hospital stay. I was about to iron his pajamas when I decided to get Ray to call his aunt at the shop and tell the family of Bobby's surgery. Shortly thereafter, Diana called the house, but as soon as I answered, she hung up. Ten minutes later, she called back. I let Ray answer, but I picked up the other receiver.

Diana asked Ray if I was in the house. He told her that I was.

"Do you see what she is doing to your dad?" she went on. "She is trying to kill him. She cannot wait for him to die so she can take over."

I was shocked. Diana was speaking like that to a child of just fourteen. After the call, I began crying and had to call Jamaica to talk to my family and let some of the emotion out.

I gave the clothes to the boys to take to their dad and decided once and for all that I had to stay away from that situation.

I went to get a manicure and, while there, I decided not to go to work that night. Instead, I decided to go up to the hospital. I put myself together nicely and my cousin joined me on the trip.

Lying in his hospital bed, Bobby was still asleep. I sat quietly at the head of his bed, while my cousin, Mike sat at

the foot. Ray was there with us, too. Apparently the rest of the family had been there, but had left before I arrived.

As the evening progressed, Pam came in and said hello to me, spoke to her brother for a couple of minutes, then left. Minutes later, Diana came in, then went to the other side of the bed and talked to him.

"Thank God, you nuh dead!" she said.

I looked at Mike and smiled.

Diana shot me an angry look.

"You tan deh laugh."

I looked her straight in the eyes, saying, "You have five minutes to visit. I am Mrs. Gardner and I am in charge, so use your five minutes wisely."

Her face turned red, and she tried to argue with me.

"If you cause any disturbance, I will have the guards remove you!"

I told her exactly what I thought of her, and what I was all about. She stayed for one hour more, then left with Ray.

I felt better having confronted her.

Later, Verona came to visit, too. Judging from the evil eyes she gave me, she had heard Diana's story. Her visit was short and pleasant.

After that day, Ray barely spoke to me, and no longer called my home. I assumed that Diana had filled his head with nasty ideas about me after our confrontation at the hospital. Raymond, of course, had already written me off, but it really hurt when Ray did, too.

The day came for me to go to Jamaica. Bobby was still in the hospital. I had visited a few times and blamed him for what I had been through with his sisters. I told him that if he had been truthful with them, they would have

realized there was no need to be angry with me.

Lorrie and I went to Jamaica. Lorrie went for two weeks and I went for three. We had a quiet, but great vacation. My brother, Gavin, took a week off from work to give us a tour of the island. But when Lorrie was meant to return, she found she was unable to. They had stolen her passport and papers, meaning she now had only a one-way ticket.

Peter, my brother-in-law, had to take two days to get Lorrie's birth certificate and passport before she could return. When she finally got them, we travelled from Montego Bay, Spanish Town to Kingston, in a race against time. We got in touch with the president of Air Canada, whom I had met before. In the end, Lorrie got a flight out and did not have to pay extra.

My problems, on the other hand, were in Kitchener. My husband, along with the others, was very nasty talking about my family. He had spread the word that Lorrie was having problems, and made it sound like it was something to do with my family.

Lorrie was upset that the news spread that she did not have a good time on her holiday. I was upset about all the gossip.

I finished my vacation by spending time with my dad. I told him about my separation from Bobby and the treatment he and his family were giving me. On his porch in the country, he took me by the hands and prayed for me. I reassured him that I would be okay, and that if ever things got too bad, I would return to Jamaica.

Chapter Thirteen

"Don't allow people to take advantage of you, because you are of great value."

When I returned to Canada after the vacation in Jamaica, I heard so many more things that Bobby had been saying about me. Before leaving, I had told my friend Jean about Bobby's illness, and told her to call when he was discharged. When I returned, she told me that she had called him to wish him well, and he'd told her all sorts of things that I had supposedly said about her. I was, as usual, shocked. Of course I'd never said anything bad about her. Likewise, Bobby's cousin, Roger had come up to visit with his wife, and Bobby had also told stories of all the things I'd said about them. Roger's wife was so hurt that she cried. She thought our friendship was a lie.

When I heard about this, I called her immediately. She was a bit withdrawn. I told her that I heard about the scandal, and that I'd said nothing of the sort. Still, there was audible pain in her voice.

Once again, Bobby had disappointed me. This man had also called my best friend, Sofia, who was very supportive and close to me. He spun the same story with her, reporting that I'd said things

I never had. Thank goodness, Sofia knew better. She told him that she would stick by me, because she knew how he was trying to distance everyone from me. She rebuked him in the name of the Lord.

Eventually, I confronted Bobby, telling him that I knew what he'd done, and that I didn't like it. Then I kept my distance. He kept calling me, apologizing.

"We can make it together," he would say.

I was so hurt by everything that he'd done, that I knew I did not want to run back into the marriage without counselling. I told him that if he was not completely honest in our therapy sessions, I would forget about the marriage. He agreed.

Counselling was good for us. I spoke about the hurtful things he'd done, and

the lies he'd told to friends and to the children. My skin crawled with the thoughts of such accusations. I told them, especially Raymond on different occasions to leave.

What mother, I ask, with troubled children and without the support of their father, could cope the way I did?

Life was not perfect, but our counseling sessions seemed successful. It seemed, once again, that we could live, respect, and appreciate one another. In the end, we decided to give the marriage another try.

One day, Raymond called me at my apartment, for just the second time since I'd moved out. The first time had been to help him with a school project; the second was to tell me that he'd been accepted into college. He knew I would be happy for him, and I was. Later, Bobby told me that

he could not afford to send Raymond to school, because it was out of town. I told Bobby that I would move home earlier than planned, and we would do this together. I told him that I had put a lot of effort in helping him reach his current position. Even though, he had treated me badly, I was still willing to help him go the distance.

I moved home at the beginning of June 1994. Bobby paid Raymond's tuition, while I paid his room and board. We, both took him to the college for orientation, and to look for a place for him to stay. He would be moving two and a half hours away from home.

Although we did our best financially, Raymond still came home every weekend. Each time he came, the transportation cost eighty dollars. Some Mondays, I drove him back, even if I'd just finished a twelve-hour shift.

After the first year, Raymond decided not to return to college. We have no idea whether or not he failed, as he refused to show us any result. After that, he took a year off and did not want to work over summer. We fought a lot that summer. While he had been away at college, I had cosigned on a loan of four thousand dollars, just for spending money for him. We paid all his school fees, as well as his living expenses, and still he spent everything. I was disappointed in him, but a man had to do what a man had to do. Raymond didn't want to go to school or find a job, instead staying in bed all day. I was becoming very frustrated. It seemed that he could not talk without being rude. He told me not to worry about him anymore, because he wouldn't ask me for anything again. Most days, I felt like crying. It was painful to see him waste his young life.

The conflict with him continued until he got a job as a security guard at his dad's workplace. But still, he would not go to work if he did not feel up to it, and was often warned about being fired from the agency. I encouraged him to seek help. It was very difficult to watch.

Chapter Fourteen

"Success does not come to you,
you go for it."

In 1996, Raymond was accepted into another college to study a different topic. I told him that he was on his own, and needed to finance his studies himself. He got a loan from the government. I along with my friend, Karen, I moved him down into a place where he was boarding with two girls. After the first month, he started call-

ing me late night, saying he thought that things would not work out this time either. He was not getting along with his roommates and wanted to come home.

That December he came home, with the expectation that he would find a new place and return in January 1997. But, he never went back.

In September of that year, I paid the term fee so that he could return to school, but by October, he still hadn't left. Eventually, he rented himself a basement apartment, and I rented a truck to move him in. Wendy helped to drive. Over the summer, Raymond had not paid anything on the loan I'd cosigned for him, and also hadn't gone to school. Because he was home, he would intercept all the letters from the bank, and then credit bureau would call, having not received any response from us.

In July 1997, a few weeks before I went home to start my house in Jamaica, the credit bureau called me and told me that we owed four thousand dollars. After the bank had failed to get a response from us, they had written to us. Little did I know, Raymond had hidden the letters. At that time, they gave us just four hours to pay or else we would be arrested and placed in prison for seven years. I made an arrangement and paid it.

"Do you know how angry and disappointed I am that you would do something like that?" I said to Raymond when I saw him.

But he just stared back at me and smiled.

I signed his rent lease for him anyway, and his dad thought I was crazy. Once more, Raymond, went to college

for a single term and then came home. He did so many terrible things during that time. He stole my credit card and maxed it out. He tore up the bills for three months. He snuck into my drawer and stole US dollars that I'd been saving for months. Yet, despite all those cruel acts, I still allowed him to drive my car to work, even when he refused to put five dollars of gas in it, or wash it. He used to drive the car until it ran out of gas, then take the bus and expect one of us to go and pick the vehicle up, refill it, and offer it to him again. When confronted, he was snarky and rude.

We had a conversation with him when I was at the end of my rope. But after explaining everything to him, he simply stared in my eyes and said, "I have nothing to say to you."

I decided that if he were going to continue disrespecting me, he'd have to move

out. No matter how many meetings we had with him, his attitude remained the same. He never said anything to me.

I became depressed. When I could not sleep, I would sit and talk to my cousin until the early hours of the morning. Raymond, while pretending to be asleep, would creep out and sit on the staircase in the dark, listening to my conversations. I knew he had to go. He would not even listen to Bobby. In the end, I gave him one month to move out.

He was twenty-three years old by that time.

Over the course of the month, Raymond did not change his attitude, nor did he try to find anywhere to move. No matter how many times I reminded him, he continued to ignore me. I became scared to sleep in the house alone with him, because I feared the things he might do to me.

After his month was up, and he was still there, I called the police and explained the situation. They came to the house and spoke to him, and he left. Bobby wasn't involved in the decision to call the cops and get him out, but he supported it because he knew how difficult Raymond had been.

After Raymond left, we heard nothing from him. I lay awake for two nights until I heard that he was okay. One month later, I left for Jamaica and Raymond moved back home with Ray. Before we left, Bobby had told Ray that he should not open the door if Raymond tried to come home, but I'd told him to let his brother in.

Eventually, Raymond decided to talk to us. We had another family meeting and he agreed that he would respect me and my property. To this day, we still have our differences. I know he

will never like me, but he must respect me as the mother I have been to him. I gave him his driving lessons along with his instructor. I gave him more than I ever gave to Ray, but it was not and will never be enough for him. Once, he told me that I was the cause of him not graduating from college.

Progressively, things at home got better. I taught Ray to drive and paid the driving school to teach him how to parallel park. Just like with Raymond, Bobby never gave Ray a single driving lesson. He totally refused to teach his sons how to drive; but I took Ray to take the test, and he passed on his first attempt. I was so proud of him.

In July of 1997, we started to dig the foundations of our house in Jamaica. Bobby and I were very happy. I had to be there for Marlene's wedding at the

same time; it was one that I did not want to miss, but I didn't want to go to the reception because I didn't want anyone to worry about where to seat me. I prayed about it and had sleepless nights worrying about what to do, but the answer I received was always to go to the ceremony, but not the reception. That's exactly what I did, and I was very pleased.

On the surface, things continued to be fine. I still felt very depressed when winter arrived, especially over Christmas time. I still missed having my family around. Even though my friends included me in their family Christmases, I still felt as if I was missing out.

At that time, I was off from work due to being unwell, but over that time I spent time thinking about faith, and I realized how thankful I was that God was such a strong force in my life. By that point, my

family relationships had stabilized, and there was little difficulty in dealing with Ray and Raymond. Whenever Raymond tried to step out of line, I prayed to God for strength, and eventually he would relent. I spent several hours on my knees each day, until my knees became sore. Feeling lonely once again, I suddenly had the urge to adopt a baby girl.

Though Ray was attentive with me, Bobby was always tired from working overtime, and Raymond only spoke to me when he needed help. I knew what Bobby's answer would be if I brought up my new desire, so I kept it to myself. I suggested it to Ray, but he said he thought we didn't have enough money to adopt another child. Still, I thought about it constantly.

Raymond found a girlfriend and got a full-time job. Ray started col-

lege, bought his own car and worked part-time.

Within a few years, Raymond had fallen in love with his girlfriend, whose name was Debbie. I wasn't too pleased about her, but Raymond was very happy. I did not want to discourage him as he seemed to enjoy his time with her. Soon, Raymond proposed to her and a year later, they were married. My family from Jamaica came in full support of the union. The wedding was fantastic, the best I have ever attended. On that day, I could see that the best was yet to come for them.

Ray was also very focused and I prayed that God would send him a great spouse and that he would come to focus on God.

Chapter Fifteen

*"The quality of a person's life is
in direct proportion to their
commitment to excellence, regardless
of their chosen field of endeavour."*

After two and a half hours in the auditorium, the audience was still listening intently to Mrs. Black-Gardner.

"Before I conclude," she said, breaking out of her story for a moment. "I pray that each couple sitting before me will recognize that no relationship is

perfect, but is rather a work in progress. You must do everything in your power to make it work."

~~~

After Raymond's wedding, Bobby and I returned to Jamaica and continued to work on our house. I got a lot of support from my brother-in-law, Peter, whose own house was halfway to being complete. Seeing that our own home would take some time, he made some adjustments to the plans of our house, building a small apartment into his design. I was delighted. It meant that when we visited Jamaica, we could stay in the small apartment while the main house was under construction. Bobby and I bought a bed, a burner, and a mini-refrigerator to make the space more comfortable.

When we returned to Canada, I worked harder than ever before. I was

anxious to see my house in Jamaica completed.

Raymond and Debbie seemed to be happily married and adjusting well to their new life, but within a few months, he started calling me late at night, complaining of challenges he was facing with Debbie. He was ready to give up on it, but I would pray for him and read the Bible to him over the phone, encouraging him to make the effort. By this point in our lives, he was very open with me and was willing to speak openly about his issues. After all our years of conflict, I felt overwhelmed that he was even willing to have a conversation with me.

At that time, Bobby and I had to travel to Jamaica often to check the progress of our dream home. On the next visit, the house was completely finished. I was thrilled by the warm welcome my family gave us, coming

to the house and preparing a big meal. They had put in a huge effort to make the house feel warm and welcoming. Together, we decided to dedicate the house to the Lord and held our first Christmas party there. I organized everything and allowed my family to bring different dishes to share. After a wonderful meal, we played card games, board games, and dominoes.

A few years later, I fell ill and became very weak. Bobby was not the type of person who liked to do anything in the kitchen, but he started to cook for me. He refused to leave the house if I was not able to go with him. I was so happy to see his progress and how he had changed in a positive way over the years. He would prepare my meals and give me it in bed and give me a kiss on my forehead. He never wanted to leave me alone, and would do everything in the bedroom, not wanting to miss a moment by my side.

One day, I said to Bobby that I knew I was going to be fine. He held my hands and looked deep in my eyes, saying, "J, I wouldn't want to miss a moment of you."

Gently, he rubbed my hands and feet.

"As I am closing my speech," said Mrs. Black-Gardner. "I want to remind you that in every relationship there are challenges. You have to know what it is you want from your relationship. Let God be the center of your marriage, and you must learn to communicate and work with each other if you want the union to survive the pressures of life."

With that, the crowd rose to its feet in a standing ovation. Mrs. Black-Garden bowed her head and walked graciously from the platform.

Brian and Rose-Marie were inspired by the story, and wanted the best for their relationship.

On the way home from the event, they could not help but talk about the direction in which their own union was headed. They resolved to love, respect, and cherish each other, and suddenly had bright hopes for the future.

By the time Rose-Marie arrived home, both her sister and her aunt were asleep.

The following morning, she got up early. She had an appointment to have her hair and nails done in preparation for her birthday. Rose-Marie was getting excited because she had no idea what Brian had in store for her.

She bounced downstairs, feeling perky.

"Good Morning, Auntie!" she said in a high-pitched voice.

"I see you had a wonderful evening! You seem in good spirits!" her aunt replied.

"Yes, Auntie!" Rose-Marie chuckled, and went off to the salon happily.

While at the hairdresser, Rose-Marie called Brian, but wasn't responding. After two hours at the hairdresser, she felt satisfied, and continued on to the nail technician. Once again, she tried to contact Brian, but there was still no response. By that evening, she was worried. She went home upset, and didn't want to eat anything. When she went up to her bedroom, the tears began to well up in her eyes. She could not believe that Brian had ignored her the whole day, even after what they had heard and said the night before. That night, as many thoughts flashed behind her eyes, Rose-Marie cried herself to sleep.

The following morning, Rose-Marie was shocked as soon as she opened her eyes. Her room was completely decorated with balloons, and twelve red roses lay beside her on the bed. She was overwhelmed with emotion. She got up and ran downstairs, looking for Brian, but he was nowhere to be seen.

She called him and he answered the phone, singing, "Happy Birthday to you!"

"Thanks, hon! I should have known!" she answered, her eyes filling with tears of happiness.

That afternoon, Brian came to pick her up for a birthday picnic in the park. Once there, they spread towels on the grass and ate delicious food, and spoke once more about Mrs. Black-Gardner. After passing a lovely afternoon, they decided to pack up their things and head home.

As they walked back to the car, Brian accidentally stepped on Rose-Marie's left

foot. He stopped, bent down, and began dusting off her shoe, apologizing. Then, suddenly he raised his head and looked into her eyes. Adjusting his position to one knee, he reached into his pocket.

"Rose-Marie, you are an amazing young lady. I love and care for you. I enjoy every moment with you as a friend, but I want to be more than a friend to you. I want to be the man of your life, for the rest of our lives, until death, do us part. I want us to argue with each other, smile together, and embrace until we are old and gray. I want to experience everything in my life with you by my side. Will you be my wife?"

Rose-Marie tried hard to fight back the tears, but the emotions were flooding through her. She began crying, shaking, and giggling like a young girl.

Brian revealed a small black box and opened it towards Rose-Marie. He reached for Rose-Marie's left hand and waited for her response, but she was speechless.

Rose-Marie felt as if her knees were buckling beneath her.

After what seemed like an eternity to Brian, she spread the fingers of her left hand wide apart and extended them towards him.

"Yes! Yes, Brian. I will!"

Brian rose from his knee and embraced Rose-Marie. They held one another close, and kissed passionately. Deep in his heart, Brian knew he had done the right thing, and he was very, very happy.

The End

In loving memory of

my dear aunt...

Aunt Jennifer

1956 - 2012

About the Author

Janeisha Hill grew up in Montego Bay, St. James. She has a Bachelor's Degree in Primary Education from the Northern Caribbean University. She currently teaches at a noble institution in the city of Montego Bay. In her leisure time, she enjoys singing spending

time with children, painting and writing. The Power of Love and Forgiveness is her first novel. She is a passionate writer and looks forward to publish similar books.

Social Media Contact of Author, Janeisha Hill

Website: www.janeishahill.com
Facebook: @HillJaneisha
Instagram: @janeishahill
Twitter: @JaneishaHill

www.ingramcontent.com/pod-product-compliance
Lightning Source LLC
Chambersburg PA
CBHW070116300326
41934CB00035B/1311